# FINANCIAL MANAGEMENT

:: Author ::

## GANESHBHAI C. NARBHAVAR

(M.COM., B.ED., G-SET)

PUBLISHED BY

The New Era International Publishing House
HQ. At & Po. Chaveli., Ta- Chansma,
Dist- Patan, North Gujarat, India, Asia.
www.iphouseindia.com

**Financial Management**

First Publication: 14th FEBRUARY, 2015

Copyright: Author
**(c) GANESHBHAI C. NARBHAVAR**

ISBN:- 978-15-08712-27-5

Price: Rs.750/- INDIA
$ 15 OUTSIDE INDIA

**PUBLISHED BY**

**The New Era International Publishing House
HQ. At & Po. Chaveli., Ta- Chansma,
Dist- Patan, North Gujarat, India, Asia.
www.iphouseindia.com**

*Dedicated to my Parents*

# An Overview of Contents

# Financial Management - Meaning, Objectives and Functions

## Meaning of Financial Management

Financial Management means planning, organizing, directing and controlling the financial activities such as procurement and utilization of funds of the enterprise. It means applying general management principles to financial resources of the enterprise.

## Scope/Elements

Investment decisions includes investment in fixed assets (called as capital budgeting). Investment in current assets are also a part of investment decisions called as working capital decisions.

**Financial decisions** - They relate to the raising of finance from various resources which will depend upon decision on type of source, period of financing, cost of financing and the returns thereby.

**Dividend decision** - The finance manager has to take decision with regards to the net profit distribution. Net profits are generally divided into two:

**Dividend for shareholders-** Dividend and the rate of it has to be decided.

**Retained profits-** Amount of retained profits has to be finalized which will depend upon expansion and diversification plans of the enterprise.

## Objectives of Financial Management

The financial management is generally concerned with procurement, allocation and control of financial resources of a concern. The objectives can be-

To ensure regular and adequate supply of funds to the concern.

To ensure adequate returns to the shareholders which will depend upon the earning capacity, market price of the share, expectations of the shareholders.

To ensure optimum funds utilization. Once the funds are procured, they should be utilized in maximum possible way at least cost.

To ensure safety on investment, i.e, funds should be invested in safe ventures so that adequate rate of return can be achieved.

To plan a sound capital structure-There should be sound and fair composition of capital so that a balance is maintained between debt and equity capital.

**Functions of Financial Management**

Estimation of capital requirements: A finance manager has to make estimation with regards to capital requirements of the company. This will depend upon expected costs and profits and future programmes and policies of a concern. Estimations have to be made in an adequate manner which increases earning capacity of enterprise.

Determination of capital composition: Once the estimation have been made, the capital structure have to be decided. This involves short- term and long- term debt equity analysis. This will depend upon the proportion of equity capital a company is possessing and additional funds which have to be raised from outside parties.

Choice of sources of funds: For additional funds to be procured, a company has many choices like-

**Issue of shares and debentures**

Loans to be taken from banks and financial institutions

Public deposits to be drawn like in form of bonds.

Choice of factor will depend on relative merits and demerits of each source and period of financing.

**Investment of funds:** The finance manager has to decide to allocate funds into profitable ventures so that there is safety on investment and regular returns is possible.

**Disposal of surplus:** The net profits decision have to be made by the finance manager. This can be done in two ways:

**Dividend declaration-** It includes identifying the rate of dividends and other benefits like bonus.

**Retained profits** - The volume has to be decided which will depend upon expansional, innovational, diversification plans of the company.

**Management of cash:** Finance manager has to make decisions with regards to cash management. Cash is required for many purposes like payment of wages and salaries, payment of electricity and water bills, payment to creditors, meeting current liabilities, maintenance of enough stock, purchase of raw materials, etc.

**Financial controls:** The finance manager has not only to plan, procure and utilize the funds but he also has to exercise control over finances. This can be done through many techniques like ratio analysis, financial forecasting, cost and profit control, etc.

## Financial Planning - Definition, Objectives and Importance

### Definition of Financial Planning

Financial Planning is the process of estimating the capital required and determining it's competition. It is the process of framing financial policies in relation to procurement, investment and administration of funds of an enterprise.

### Objectives of Financial Planning

Financial Planning has got many objectives to look forward to:

a. Determining capital requirements- This will depend upon factors like cost of current and fixed assets, promotional expenses and long- range planning. Capital requirements have to be looked with both aspects: short- term and long- term requirements.

b. Determining capital structure- The capital structure is the composition of capital, i.e., the relative kind and proportion of capital required in the business. This includes decisions of debt- equity ratio- both short-term and long- term.

c. Framing financial policies with regards to cash control, lending, borrowings, etc.

d. A finance manager ensures that the scarce financial resources are maximally utilized in the best possible manner at least cost in order to get maximum returns on investment.

## Importance of Financial Planning

Financial Planning is process of framing objectives, policies, procedures, programmes and budgets regarding the financial activities of a concern. This ensures effective and adequate financial and investment policies. The importance can be outlined as-

1. Adequate funds have to be ensured.

2. Financial Planning helps in ensuring a reasonable balance between outflow and inflow of funds so that stability is maintained.

3. Financial Planning ensures that the suppliers of funds are easily investing in companies which exercise financial planning.

4. Financial Planning helps in making growth and expansion programmes which helps in long-run survival of the company.

5. Financial Planning reduces uncertainties with regards to changing market trends which can be faced easily through enough funds.

6. Financial Planning helps in reducing the uncertainties which can be a hindrance to growth of the company. This helps in ensuring stability an d profitability in concern.

## Finance Functions

The following explanation will help in understanding each finance function in detail

## Investment Decision

One of the most important finance functions is to

intelligently allocate capital to long term assets. This activity is also known as capital budgeting. It is important to allocate capital in those long term assets so as to get maximum yield in future. Following are the two aspects of investment decision

    a. Evaluation of new investment in terms of profitability

    b. Comparison of cut off rate against new investment and prevailing investment.

Since the future is uncertain therefore there are difficulties in calculation of expected return. Along with uncertainty comes the risk factor which has to be taken into consideration. This risk factor plays a very significant role in calculating the expected return of the prospective investment. Therefore while considering investment proposal it is important to take into consideration both expected return and the risk involved.

Investment decision not only involves allocating capital to long term assets but also involves decisions of using funds which are obtained by selling those assets which become less profitable and less productive. It wise decisions to decompose depreciated assets which are not adding value and utilize those funds in securing other beneficial assets. An opportunity cost of capital needs to be calculating while dissolving such assets. The correct cut off rate is calculated by using this opportunity cost of the required rate of return (RRR)

**Financial Decision**

Financial decision is yet another important function which a financial manger must perform. It is important to make wise decisions about when, where and how should a business acquire funds. Funds can be acquired through many ways and channels. Broadly speaking a correct ratio of an equity and debt has to be maintained. This mix of equity capital and debt is known as a firm's capital structure. A firm tends to benefit most when the market value of a company's share maximizes this not only is a sign of growth for the firm but also maximizes shareholders wealth. On the other hand the use of debt affects the risk and return of a shareholder. It is more risky though it may increase the return on equity funds. A sound financial structure is said to be one which aims at maximizing shareholders return with minimum risk. In such a scenario the market value of the firm will maximize and hence an optimum capital structure would be achieved. Other than equity and debt there are several other tools which are used in deciding a firm capital structure.

## Dividend Decision

Earning profit or a positive return is a common aim of all the businesses. But the key function a financial manger performs in case of profitability is to decide whether to distribute all the profits to the shareholder or retain all the profits or distribute part of the profits to the shareholder and retain the other half in the business. It's the financial manager's responsibility to decide a optimum dividend policy which maximizes the market value of the firm. Hence an optimum dividend payout ratio is calculated. It is a common practice to pay regular dividends in case of profitability Another way is to issue bonus shares to existing shareholders.

## Liquidity Decision

It is very important to maintain a liquidity position of a firm to avoid insolvency. Firm's profitability, liquidity and risk all are associated with the investment in current assets. In order to maintain a tradeoff between profitability and liquidity it is important to invest sufficient funds in current assets. But since current assets do not earn anything for business therefore a proper calculation must be done before investing in current assets. Current assets should properly be valued and disposed of from time to time once they become non profitable. Currents assets must be used in times of liquidity problems and times of insolvency.

## The Role of the Finance Function in Organizational Processes
### The Finance Function and the Project Office

Contemporary organizations need to practice cost control if they are to survive the recessionary times. Given the fact that many top tier companies are currently mired in low growth and less activity situations, it is imperative that they control their costs as much as possible. This can happen only when the finance function in these companies is diligent and has a hawk eye towards the costs being incurred. Apart from this, companies also have to introduce efficiencies in the way their processes operate and this is another role for the finance function in modern day organizations. Further, there must be synergies between the various processes and this is where the finance function can play a critical role. Lest one thinks that the finance function, which is essentially a support function, has to do this all by themselves, it is useful to note that, many contemporary organizations have dedicated project office teams for each division, which perform this function. In other words, whereas the finance function oversees the organizational processes at a macro level, the project office teams indulge in the same at the micro level. This is the reason why finance and project budgeting and cost control have assumed significance because after all, companies exist to make profits and finance is the lifeblood that determines whether organizations are profitable or failures.

## The Pension Fund Management and Tax Activities of the Finance Function

The next role of the finance function is in payroll, claims processing, and acting as the repository of pension schemes and gratuity. If the US follow the 401(k) rule and the finance function manages the defined benefit and defined contribution schemes, in India it is the EPF or the Employee Provident Funds that are managed by the finance function. Of course, only large organizations have dedicated EPF trusts to take care of these aspects and the norm in most other organizations is to act as facilitators for the EPF scheme with the local or regional PF (Provident Fund) commissioner. The third aspect of the role of the finance function is to manage the taxes and their collection at source from the employees. Whereas in the US, TDS or Tax Deduction at Source works differently from other countries, in India and much of the Western world, it is mandatory for organizations to deduct tax at source from the employees commensurate with their pay and benefits. The finance function also has to coordinate with the tax authorities and hand out the annual tax statements that form the basis of the employee's tax returns. Often, this is a sensitive and critical process since the tax rules mandate very strict principles for generating the tax statements.

## Payroll, Claims Processing, and Automation

We have discussed the pension fund management and the tax deduction. The other role of the finance function is to process payroll and associated benefits in time and in tune with the regulatory requirements. Further, claims made by the employees with respect to medical, and transport allowances have to be processed by the finance function. Often, many organizations automate this routine activity wherein the use of

ERP (Enterprise Resource Planning) software and financial workflow automation software make the job and the task of claims processing easier. Having said that, it must be remembered that the finance function has to do its due diligence on the claims being submitted to ensure that bogus claims and suspicious activities are found out and stopped. This is the reason why many organizations have experienced chartered accountants and financial professionals in charge of the finance function so that these aspects can be managed professionally and in a trustworthy manner. The key aspect here is that the finance function must be headed by persons of high integrity and trust that the management reposes in them must not be misused. In conclusion, the finance function though a non-core process in many organizations has come to occupy a place of prominence because of these aspects.

## Role of a Financial Manager

Financial activities of a firm is one of the most important and complex activities of a firm. Therefore in order to take care of these activities a financial manager performs all the requisite financial activities.

A financial manger is a person who takes care of all the important financial functions of an organization. The person in charge should maintain a far sightedness in order to ensure that the funds are utilized in the most efficient manner. His actions directly affect the Profitability, growth and goodwill of the firm.

**Following are the main functions of a Financial Manager:**

### 1. Raising of Funds

In order to meet the obligation of the business it is important to have enough cash and liquidity. A firm can raise funds by the way of equity and debt. It is the responsibility of a financial manager to decide the ratio between debt and equity. It is important to maintain a good balance between equity and debt.

### 2. Allocation of Funds

Once the funds are raised through different channels the next important function is to allocate the funds. The funds should be allocated in such a manner that they are optimally used. In order to allocate funds in the best possible manner the following point must be considered

- The size of the firm and its growth capability
- Status of assets whether they are long term or short tem
- Mode by which the funds are raised.

These financial decisions directly and indirectly influence other managerial activities. Hence formation of a good asset mix and proper allocation of funds is one of the most important activity

## 3. Profit Planning

Profit earning is one of the prime functions of any business organization. Profit earning is important for survival and sustenance of any organization. Profit planning refers to proper usage of the profit generated by the firm. Profit arises due to many factors such as pricing, industry competition, state of the economy, mechanism of demand and supply, cost and output. A healthy mix of variable and fixed factors of production can lead to an increase in the profitability of the firm. Fixed costs are incurred by the use of fixed factors of production such as land and machinery. In order to maintain a tandem it is important to continuously value the depreciation cost of fixed cost of production. An opportunity cost must be calculated in order to replace those factors of production which has gone thrown wear and tear. If this is not noted then these fixed cost can cause huge fluctuations in profit.

## 4. Understanding Capital Markets

Shares of a company are traded on stock exchange and there is a continuous sale and purchase of securities. Hence a clear understanding of capital market is an important function of a financial manager. When securities are traded on stock market there involves a huge amount of risk involved. Therefore a financial manger understands and calculates the risk involved in this trading of shares and debentures. Its on the discretion of a financial manager as to how distribute the profits. Many investors do not like the firm to distribute the profits amongst share holders as dividend instead invest in the business itself to enhance growth. The practices of a financial manager directly impact the operation in

## Capital Structure - Meaning and Factors Determining Capital Structure

### Meaning of Capital Structure

Capital Structure is referred to as the ratio of different kinds of securities raised by a firm as long-term finance. The capital structure involves two decisions-

a. Type of securities to be issued are equity shares, preference shares and long term borrowings (Debentures).

b. Relative ratio of securities can be determined by process of capital gearing. On this basis, the companies are divided into two-

   i.   Highly geared companies - Those companies whose proportion of equity capitalization is small.

   ii.   Low geared companies - Those companies whose equity capital dominates total capitalization.

For instance - There are two companies A and B. Total capitalization amounts to be Rs. 200,000 in each case. The ratio of equity capital to total capitalization in company A is Rs. 50,000, while in company B, ratio of equity capital is Rs.

150,000 to total capitalization, i.e, in Company A, proportion is 25% and in company B, proportion is 75%. In such cases, company A is considered to be a highly geared company and company B is low geared company.

**Factors Determining Capital Structure**

1. **Trading on Equity-** The word "equity" denotes the ownership of the company. Trading on equity means taking advantage of equity share capital to borrowed funds on reasonable basis. It refers to additional profits that equity shareholders earn because of issuance of debentures and preference shares. It is based on the thought that if the rate of dividend on preference capital and the rate of interest on borrowed capital is lower than the general rate of company's earnings, equity shareholders are at advantage which means a company should go for a judicious blend of preference shares, equity shares as well as debentures. Trading on equity becomes more important when expectations of shareholders are high.

2. **Degree of control-** In a company, it is the directors who are so called elected representatives of equity

shareholders. These members have got maximum voting rights in a concern as compared to the preference shareholders and debenture holders. Preference shareholders have reasonably less voting rights while debenture holders have no voting rights. If the company's management policies are such that they want to retain their voting rights in their hands, the capital structure consists of debenture holders and loans rather than equity shares.

3. **Flexibility of financial plan-** In an enterprise, the capital structure should be such that there is both contractions as well as relaxation in plans. Debentures and loans can be refunded back as the time requires. While equity capital cannot be refunded at any point which provides rigidity to plans. Therefore, in order to make the capital structure possible, the company should go for issue of debentures and other loans.

4. **Choice of investors-** The company's policy generally is to have different categories of investors for securities. Therefore, a capital structure should give enough choice to all kind of investors to invest. Bold and adventurous investors generally go for equity shares and loans and

debentures are generally raised keeping into mind conscious investors.

5. **Capital market condition-** In the lifetime of the company, the market price of the shares has got an important influence. During the depression period, the company's capital structure generally consists of debentures and loans. While in period of boons and inflation, the company's capital should consist of share capital generally equity shares.

6. **Period of financing-** When company wants to raise finance for short period, it goes for loans from banks and other institutions; while for long period it goes for issue of shares and debentures.

7. **Cost of financing-** In a capital structure, the company has to look to the factor of cost when securities are raised. It is seen that debentures at the time of profit earning of company prove to be a cheaper source of finance as compared to equity shares where equity shareholders demand an extra share in profits.

8. **Stability of sales-** An established business which has a growing market and high sales turnover, the company is in position to meet fixed commitments. Interest on

debentures has to be paid regardless of profit. Therefore, when sales are high, thereby the profits are high and company is in better position to meet such fixed commitments like interest on debentures and dividends on preference shares. If company is having unstable sales, then the company is not in position to meet fixed obligations. So, equity capital proves to be safe in such cases.

9. **Sizes of a company-** Small size business firms capital structure generally consists of loans from banks and retained profits. While on the other hand, big companies having goodwill, stability and an established profit can easily go for issuance of shares and debentures as well as loans and borrowings from financial institutions. The bigger the size, the wider is total capitalization.

## Capitalization in Finance

## What is Capitalization

Capitalization comprises of share capital, debentures, loans, free reserves, etc. Capitalization represents permanent investment in companies excluding long-term loans.

Capitalization can be distinguished from capital structure. Capital structure is a broad term and it deals with qualitative aspect of finance. While capitalization is a narrow term and it deals with the quantitative aspect.

Capitalization is generally found to be of following types-

- Normal
- Over
- Under

## Overcapitalization

Overcapitalization is a situation in which actual profits of a company are not sufficient enough to pay interest on debentures, on loans and pay dividends on shares over a period of time. This situation arises when the company raises more capital than required. A part of capital always remains idle. With a result, the rate of return shows a declining trend. The causes can be-

1. **High promotion cost-** When a company goes for high promotional expenditure, i.e., making contracts, canvassing, underwriting commission, drafting of documents, etc. and the actual returns are not adequate in

proportion to high expenses, the company is over-capitalized in such cases.

2. **Purchase of assets at higher prices-** When a company purchases assets at an inflated rate, the result is that the book value of assets is more than the actual returns. This situation gives rise to over-capitalization of company.

3. **A company's floatation n boom period-** At times company has to secure it's solvency and thereby float in boom periods. That is the time when rate of returns are less as compared to capital employed. This results in actual earnings lowering down and earnings per share declining.

4. **Inadequate provision for depreciation-** If the finance manager is unable to provide an adequate rate of depreciation, the result is that inadequate funds are available when the assets have to be replaced or when they become obsolete. New assets have to be purchased at high prices which prove to be expensive.

5. **Liberal dividend policy-** When the directors of a company liberally divide the dividends into the shareholders, the result is inadequate retained profits which are very essential for high earnings of the

company. The result is deficiency in company. To fill up the deficiency, fresh capital is raised which proves to be a costlier affair and leaves the company to be over-capitalized.

6. **Over-estimation of earnings-** When the promoters of the company overestimate the earnings due to inadequate financial planning, the result is that company goes for borrowings which cannot be easily met and capital is not profitably invested. This results in consequent decrease in earnings per share.

## Effects of Overcapitalization

1. **On Shareholders-** The over capitalized companies have following disadvantages to shareholders:

   a. Since the profitability decreases, the rate of earning of shareholders also decreases.

   b. The market price of shares goes down because of low profitability.

   c. The profitability going down has an effect on the shareholders. Their earnings become uncertain.

d. With the decline in goodwill of the company, share prices decline. As a result shares cannot be marketed in capital market.

2. **On Company-**

   a. Because of low profitability, reputation of company is lowered.

   b. The company's shares cannot be easily marketed.

   c. With the decline of earnings of company, goodwill of the company declines and the result is fresh borrowings are difficult to be made because of loss of credibility.

   d. In order to retain the company's image, the company indulges in malpractices like manipulation of accounts to show high earnings.

   e. The company cuts down it's expenditure on maintainance, replacement of assets, adequate depreciation, etc.

3. **On Public-** An overcapitalized company has got many adverse effects on the public:

   a. In order to cover up their earning capacity, the management indulges in tactics like increase in prices or decrease in quality.

b. Return on capital employed is low. This gives an impression to the public that their financial resources are not utilized properly.

c. Low earnings of the company affects the credibility of the company as the company is not able to pay it's creditors on time.

d. It also has an effect on working conditions and payment of wages and salaries also lessen.

## Undercapitalization

An undercapitalized company is one which incurs exceptionally high profits as compared to industry. An undercapitalized company situation arises when the estimated earnings are very low as compared to actual profits. This gives rise to additional funds, additional profits, high goodwill, high earnings and thus the return on capital shows an increasing trend. The causes can be-

1. **Low promotion costs**
2. **Purchase of assets at deflated rates**
3. **Conservative dividend policy**
4. **Floatation of company in depression stage**
5. **High efficiency of directors**

6. **Adequate provision of depreciation**

7. **Large secret reserves are maintained.**

## Efffects of Under Capitalization

1. **On Shareholders**

   a. Company's profitability increases. As a result, rate of earnings go up.

   b. Market value of share rises.

   c. Financial reputation also increases.

   d. Shareholders can expect a high dividend.

2. **On company**

   a. With greater earnings, reputation becomes strong.

   b. Higher rate of earnings attract competition in market.

   c. Demand of workers may rise because of high profits.

   d. The high profitability situation affects consumer interest as they think that the company is overcharging on products.

3. **On Society**

a. With high earnings, high profitability, high market price of shares, there can be unhealthy speculation in stock market.

b. 'Restlessness in general public is developed as they link high profits with high prices of product.

c. Secret reserves are maintained by the company which can result in paying lower taxes to government.

d. The general public inculcates high expectations of these companies as these companies can import innovations, high technology and thereby best quality of product.

## Financial Goal - Profit vs Wealth

Every firm has a predefined goal or an objective. Therefore the most important goal of a financial manager is to increase the owner's economic welfare. Here economics welfare may refer to maximization of profit or maximization of shareholders wealth. Therefore Shareholders wealth maximization (SWM) plays a very crucial role as far as financial goals of a firm are concerned.

**Profit is the remuneration paid to the entrepreneur after**

**deduction of all expenses. Maximization of profit can be defined as maximizing the income of the firm and minimizing the expenditure**. The main responsibility of a firm is to carry out business by manufacturing goods and services and selling them in the open market. The mechanism of demand and supply in an open market determine the price of a commodity or a service. A firm can only make profit if it produces a good or delivers a service at a lower cost than what is prevailing in the market. The margin between these two prices would only increase if the firm strives to produce these goods more efficiently and at a lower price without compromising on the quality.

The demand and supply mechanism plays a very important role in determining the price of a commodity. A commodity which has a greater demand commands a higher price and hence may result in greater profits. Competition among other suppliers also effect profits. Manufacturers tends to move towards production of those goods which guarantee higher profits. Hence there comes a time when equilibrium is reached and profits are saturated.

According to Adam Smith - **business man in order to fulfill their profit motive in turn benefits the society as well**. It is seen that when a firm tends to increase profit it eventually makes use of its resources in a more effective manner. Profit is regarded as a parameter to measure firm's productivity and efficiency. Firms which tend to earn continuous profit eventually improvise their products according to the demand of the consumers. Bulk production due to massive demand leads to economies of scale which eventually reduces the cost of production. Lower cost of production directly impacts the profit margins. There are two ways to increase the profit margin due to lower cost. Firstly a firm can produce at lower sot but continue to sell at the original price, thereby increasing the revenue. Secondly a firm can reduce the final price offered to the consumer and increase its market thereby superseding its competitors.

Both ways the firm will benefit. The second way would increase its sale and market share while the first way only tend to increase its revenue. Profit is an important component of any business. Without profit earning capability it is very difficult to survive in the market. If a firm continues to earn large amount of profits then only it can manage to serve the society in the long run. Therefore profit earning capacity by a firm and public motive in some way goes hand in hand. This eventually also leads to the growth of an economy and increase in National Income due to increasing purchasing power of the consumer.

## Opportunity Cost of Capital

Opportunity cost of a capital is a term unique to economics and finance. It is unique in the sense that you will not find mention of opportunity cost of capital in the accounting books. It is not an explicit cost which is paid out of the pocket. Hence, there is no mention of this cost in the accounting records. Rather, it is an implicit cost which results out of our investment decisions. This will explain about opportunity cost of capital and how it must be used while making financial decisions:

## Alternate Uses of Money

**Opportunity cost of capital represents alternate uses of money**. Let's say, if I have a Rs.1000 to invest and I decide to invest the money in the stock market, I am committing my resources. By investing Rs.1000 in the stock market, I will now not be able to use the same Rs.1000 for any other purposes now. I must therefore ensure that I am committing my resources to the best possible project. Let's say, I have a choice between real estate and stock market investment, when I choose the stock market investment, I make it my best possible choice. Opportunity cost of capital tells us what we are foregoing to choose that best possible alternative. Opportunity cost of capital is therefore the value of the second best alternative.

## Alternate Projects Must Share Similar Risk Profile

However, **we must ensure that we compare opportunity costs of capital across similar projects**. This will ensure that we do not see a biased picture and end up choosing the wrong projects. Consider a comparison between a stock market investment and government bonds. Usually, stock markets will offer more return compared to government bonds. So, using government bonds as the opportunity cost will always make them look good. But stock market investments and government bond investments have very different risk profiles. One guarantees a fixed rate of return whereas there are no guarantees in the other. Hence, using one as the opportunity cost of capital for another will provide a skewed picture and the risky alternative will always be chosen. Hence, only projects with similar risk must be used for opportunity cost of capital calculation. This makes these calculations very subjective and open to debate.

## Alternate Uses Represent Implicit Costs

The investment decision is all about prioritizing. It is about choosing the best possible alternative. So, if we have 2 alternatives, one which offers a Rs.100 return potential whereas another which offers an Rs.80 return potential, then by choosing one alternative we are alternatively foregoing the other one. So, if we choose to get a Rs.100 return, we are foregoing the Rs.80 return. Corporate finance captures this implicit tradeoff in the expected rate of return number.

## How Opportunity Cost Helps in Decision Making ?

Opportunity cost helps in choosing the right project when faced with a variety of alternatives. Here is how the decision is affected:

- **Higher Opportunity Cost Lowers NPV:** A higher opportunity cost implies a bigger discount rate. A bigger discount rate means that the future values are worth considerably less today. This creates a situation where the NPV is lowered. A high opportunity cost of capital raises the bar for all other projects as well.

- **Only the Best Investment Has Positive NPV:** Also, we need to understand that in a given set of 2-3 investment proposals, only the best proposal will have a positive NPV. This is because the best proposal will be the opportunity cost of capital for the other projects. Since the opportunity cost of capital will be higher than the cash flows that the project has to offer, the NPV of such a project will be negative. One just needs to be careful about the risk profile of different projects to ensure an "apples to apples" comparison.

## What is Cost of Equity ? - Meaning and Concept

**Theoretical Concept**

The cost of equity concept is very important when it comes to valuing shares on the stock market. Equity, like all other investment classes expects a compensation to be paid to its investors. The problem however is that unlike debt and other classes the cost of equity is never really straightforward.

You can look at the interest rates that you are paying and you will straight away know what the cost of debt for your company is. However, the cost of equity is implied. Equity holders take the residual value that has been left from the profits. So it is not directly available.

However, for valuation purposes, the cost of equity is required. Without having the cost of equity and adding it to the discount rate, we will use a lower discount rate that does not reflect the riskiness of the investment. This may lead to selection of the wrong investments. So, this provides a basis about how we can calculate the cost of equity.

There are two methods to calculating the cost of equity. One is the method that we are about to discuss now and the other is called the "Capital Asset Pricing Model". That will be discussed in a later in the same module.

**Assumes Market Price Is Correct:**

In this method, we will begin with the assumption that the market price is correct. Now, we already know that the market price is nothing but the discounted value of all the future dividends that the company will pay, we can consider the market price to be the value of a perpetuity. Using the perpetuity formula, we can then express the market price as:

Market Price = Dividend (Next Year) / Discount Rate

**Growing Perpetuity:**

However in a perpetuity the payments remain the same throughout the life of the asset. So by using this formula, we are making the assumption that the dividends paid out across the life of the stock will be the same. Now, we know for sure that is not the case. In reality, the dividends usually grow over time. So we can use the formula for a growing perpetuity. That should give us a better approximation.

Market Price = Dividend (Next Year) / (Discount Rate – Growth Rate)

**Rearrange The Formula:**

So, now we can re-arrange this formula and solve for the discount rate. The discount rate is our cost of capital and it will be the output from the rearranged formula.

Discount Rate = {Dividend (Next Year) / Market Price} + Growth Rate

So, here it is! We have derived a formula which tells us an estimate of what is the cost of equity that is being demanded from this company by the market.

## Estimating the Growth Rate:

Since growth rate is an important component of this formula, we need to ensure that we are using the correct growth rate. We can conduct this estimation in a couple of ways.

- Firstly, we could just calculate what the growth rate has been in the past. We can understand the trend and then use the same growth rate assuming that what happened in the past will continue in the future.
- Alternatively, we could make a more educated guess. The growth rate of dividend next year is dependent on the amount that we invest in the business this year and the rate of return we should earn on that investment right. So growth rate can be derived by using this formula:

**Growth Rate = Plowback Ratio \* ROE**

Plowback ratio is the amount that the company expects to retain in the business whereas ROE is the return on equity that the company historically earns on its equity investments.

It may seem a little complex and full of formulas at the beginning. But there really is just one formula. Other formulas are used to derive the components that will be used in that single formula. So calculating the Cost of Equity that is being implied by the market price shouldn't really be that difficult.

**What is Internal Rate of Return (IRR) ?**

**The Internal Rate of Return (IRR) is another very important metric that can be used to determine whether or not a company must invest its resources in a project.** If the company does decide to invest its resources in all the projects then the IRR can help us understand what should be the priority of these projects for the company.

**What Is Internal Rate of Return (IRR) ?**

Let's understand Internal Rate of Return (IRR) with the help of an example. Let's say that we have an investment that pays Rs.10 on a Rs.100 investment. So, we can clearly see that the rate of return is 10%. This means 10% of the money invested will be recouped every single time period. But this calculation was simple because there was only one return we received and we just had to calculate its size as compared to the original investment.

Now, consider the fact that for the same Rs.100 investment, you are going to receive Rs.20 for the first 2 years, Rs.30 for the next 2 years and Rs.50 in the 5th year. So what would be the rate of return for this investment? So here we are taking a complex schedule of cash outflows and inflows and we are basically coming up with a single rate that describes the rate of return. In the above example the rate of return is 13%.

This means that if we invested Rs.100 and got a consistent rate of interest which was compounded at 13%, then that investment would be equivalent to the above investment. The above investment provides the same return as that of a bond with an annual coupon of 13%. This is the Internal Rate of Return (IRR) of the investment.

The calculation of Internal Rate of Return (IRR) with a formula is very complex and is never used in practice. We generally use financial calculators or MS Excel both of which have inbuilt IRR functions to find out the IRR.

## Relationship between the IRR and the NPV

The relationship between the IRR and the NPV is very important. In fact, it could be the defining characteristic of IRR. IRR is the rate at which NPV of the project is zero. This is clearly intuitive. Consider the fact that the rate of growth of your investment and the discount rate both will be the same in this case. Therefore they will nullify each other and the NPV will be zero at IRR.

## The Internal Rate of Return (IRR) Rule

The rule pertaining to the IRR is simple. A company must decide a hurdle IRR rate. Let's say the hurdle rate is 10%. So, the company must then choose investments that pay over 10% and must reject investments that pay less than 10%. In the above example 13% is greater than 10% and hence the investment must be selected. In case the company wants to choose between 2 projects both of which have more than 10% return, then the one with the higher Internal Rate of Return (IRR) must be selected.

The IRR metric is also flawed. But its flaws are smaller as compared to the payback period method. It is for this reason that many companies do in fact use the IRR method to decide amongst investments. It is a little bit more intuitive to use.

In the past we discussed about the concept of internal rate of return. We discussed how it could be used to make proficient investment decisions. we will see the drawbacks and pitfalls of the Internal Rate of Return (IRR) number. We will see how these problems make it a number that must be handled with care and why decisions based entirely on the IRR rule may not be good for the firm. The problems with Internal Rate of Return (IRR) are as follows:

**Problem #1: Multiple Rates of Return**

The Internal Rate of Return (IRR) is a complex mathematical formula. It takes inputs, solves a complex equation and gives out an answer. However, these answers are not correct all the time. There are some cases in which the cash flow pattern is such that the calculation of IRR actually ends up giving multiple rates. So instead of having one IRR, we would then have multiple IRR's. Sometimes the IRR number can even go in the negative indicating that the firm is actually losing value. Although, we know that this is not the case in reality.

The thumb rule is that if the cash flow patterns change signs more than ones then the firm sees more than 1 IRR. These numbers are therefore not wholly accurate. They are simply the result of a mathematical error of a complex formula. In such cases, using the NPV is a better choice.

And most projects that firms have to choose from will usually have cash flows which change signs many times. Sometimes there is a maintenance outlay required during the later life of the project. Sometimes disposing off the waste at the end of the project requires an outlay in the end. In each of these cases, Internal Rate of Return (IRR) is not a good basis for decisions.

## Problem # 2: Multiple Discount Rates

Even if the cash flow does not change signs in the middle of the project, the IRR could still be very difficult to compute and implement in reality. We must only invest if the IRR is greater than the opportunity cost of capital. But, here we are just discussing one opportunity cost of capital. Time value of money tells us that there are in fact several opportunity costs of capital, changing each year because of the effect of increasing number of years.

So, to use the IRR rule in such a case we have two choices:

1. We can use the IRR and the discount rate values for each year and make a decision
2. Alternatively, we can compute a weighted average Internal Rate of Return (IRR) and use that to make the decision

Either ways, it becomes a mathematical hassle. This is both difficult to comprehend as well as difficult to compute. It is for this reason that firms usually prefer the net present value (NPV) rule to the Internal Rate of Return (IRR) rule.

## Profit Maximization Criticisms
**Many economists have argued that profit maximization has brought about many disparities among consumers and manufacturers.** In case of perfect competition it may appear

as a legitimate and a reward for efforts but in case of imperfect competition a firm's prime objective should not be profit maximization. In olden times when there was not too much of competition selling and manufacturing goods were primarily for mutual benefit. Manufacturers didn't produce to earn profits rather produced for mutual benefit and social welfare. The aim of the single producer was to retain his position in the market and sustain growth, thereby earning some profit which would help him in maintaining his position. On the other hand in today's time the production system is dominant by two tier system of ownership and management. Ownership aims at maximizing profit and management aims at managing the system of production thereby indirectly increasing the income of the business.

These services are used by customers who in turn are forced to pay a higher price due to formation of cartels and monopoly. Not only have the customers suffered but also the employees. Employees are forced to work more than their capacity. they is made to pay in extra hours so that production can increase.

Many times manufacturers tend to produce goods which are of no use to the society and create an artificial demand for the product by rigorous marketing and advertising. They tend to make the product so tempting by packaging and labeling that its difficult for the consumer to resist. These happen mainly with products which aim to target kids and teenagers. Ad commercials and print ads tend to provide with wrong information to artificially hike the expectation of the product.

In case of oligopoly where the nature of the product is more or less same exploit the customer to the max. Since they form cartels and manipulate prices by giving very less flexibility to the consumer to negotiate or choose from the products available. In such a scenario it is the consumer who becomes prey of these activities. Profit maximization motive is continuously aiming at increasing the firm's revenue and is concentrating less on the social welfare.

Government plays a very important role in curbing this practice of charging extraordinary high prices at the cost of service or product. In fact a market which experiences a high degree of competition is likely to exploit the customer in the name of profit maximization, and on the other hand where the production of a particular product or service is limited there is a possibility to charge higher prices is greater. There are few things which need a greater clarification as far as maximization of profit is concerned

**Profit maximization objective is a little vague in terms of returns achieved by a firm in different time period. The time value of money is often ignored when measuring profit.**

It leads to uncertainty of returns. Two firms which use same technology and same factors of production may eventually earn different returns. It is due to the profit margin. It may not be legitimate if seen from a different stand point.

## 3 Modern Financial Management Techniques that Will Change Your Business

Whether you're a business or an individual, you have to find a way to manage your finances now and in the future. The cost of everything continues to increase and there's no sign that this trend of price increases will stop anytime soon. As a result, all entities have to develop a financial management system to ensure their stability for many years to come.

This system has to provide the businesses in question with enough flexibility for them to continue to grow and pay for their necessary expenses. It also has to be stringent enough to allow for money to be put away in the event of future catastrophes.

In the case of a business, all expenses have to be prioritized in the interest of spending money on the right things.

When it comes time for cost cutting measures to be implemented, they have to be come with consequences in mind. Everything that's done to cut costs has an end result once it becomes a common procedure.

You have to ponder whether you're cutting enough or you're cutting too much. Work has to be done to ensure that cutting individuals from the workforce is the last possible resort. Odds are there are expenses that can be sliced without having to touch the workforce.

Individuals in the private sector have to manage their finances in the interest of being able to acquire credit.

A person's credit score can affect every possible aspect of their life. The biggest issue currently impacting the financial future of most people is the regular use of high interest credit cards.

Most retail establishments try to push their credit card on their customers on a regular basis. These cards should only be used for small purchases that can be paid shortly after they have been completed.

Financial management is a challenge in a world where spending is seen as the key to getting ahead.

You have to exercise the utmost level of restraint if you want solvency to be in your future. Once you have established an effective budget, your worries about finances will become a thing of the past.

## Working Capital Management: Concept, Need & Determinants

Working capital could be defined as the portion of assets used in current operations. The movement of funds from working capital to income and profits and back to working capital is one of the most important characteristics of business. This cyclical operation is concerned with utilisation of funds with the hope that they will return with an additional amount called Income. If the operations of a company are to run smoothly, a proper relationship between fixed capital and current capital has to be maintained.

Sufficient liquidity is important and must be achieved and maintained to provide the funds to pay off obligations as they arise or mature. The adequacy of cash and other current assets together with their efficient handling, virtually determine the survival or demise of the company. A businessman should be able to judge the accurate requirement of working capital and should be quick enough to raise the required funds to finance the working capital needs.

Working capital is often classified as Gross Working Capital and Net Working Capital.

The former refers to the total of all Current Assets and the latter refers to the difference between Current Assets and Current Liabilities. The maintenance of a sound Working

Capital position is an important function of the Finance Department of the organisation. With the magnitude of business rising with globalisation, the quantum of working capital to be managed is on the increase. No wonder, working capital management is talked about more today than ever before. Long-term investment decisions (capital budgeting) and long-term financing decisions are characterized by the facts that they (a) generally involve large amounts of money, and (b) are relatively infrequent occurrences. Decisions that come under the heading short-term finance" are equally important, because, while typical decisions often don't involve as much money, decisions are much more frequent. This is suggested in the results of a recent survey of CFOs.

In defining short term finance, we focus on the cash flows connected with the operations of a company. Because the cash inflows and cash outflows are not synchronised, a company needs a temporary parking place for cash, which we can call a liquidity portfolio. This liquidity portfolio may consist of cash and marketable securities. Since cash flows for a company are uncertain, both in amount and timing, the amount of cash in temporary storage may not be adequate for all time periods. Thus, it is necessary to provide some backup liquidity for periods when the normal store of liquidity is insufficient. Also there is a need to move cash from one point to another within a company. We need to have internal cash flows to connect these various inflows, outflows and sources of liquidity. The cash system of a company is the mechanism that provides the linkage between cash flows. The financial manager of the company has the responsibility, at least in part, to develop and maintain the policies and procedures necessary to achieve an efficient flow of cash for the company's operations. Short term financial management thus encompasses decisions about activities that affect cash inflows, cash outflows, liquidity, backup liquidity, and internal cash flows. Many decisions of a company have a short term financial management aspect. For example, the decision to sell a bond issue in order to raise funds to finance an expansion in plant and equipment is clearly a long term decision. However, the decision on how to invest the proceeds from the bond issue until they are needed to pay for the construction is a short term financial decision.

The use of a 1-year time horizon to separate short term and long term decisions is arbitrary and, in some cases, ambiguous. To refine the definition of short term finance, it is helpful to examine the differences and interrelationships between the decisions that are classified as short term finance and those that are considered long term finance. Decisions usually classified as long term are difficult to reverse and essentially determine the basic nature of the business and how it will be carried out. Short term financial policies take the results of these decisions as a starting point and concentrate on how they can be efficiently and economically carried out. We can think of short term decisions as being more operational. Once implemented they are easier to change Importance of Working Capital Management Working capital management includes a number of aspects that make it an important topic for study, and we will now consider some of them. Surveys indicate that the largest portion of a financial manager's time is devoted to the day –by- day internal operation of the firm; this may be appropriately subsumed under the heading "working capital management." since so much time is spent on working capital decisions, it is appropriate that the subject be covered carefully in managerial finance courses.

Characteristically, current assets represent more than half the total as-sets of a business firm. Because they represent a large investment and because this investment tends to be relatively volatile, current assets are worthy of the financial manager's careful attention. Working capital management is particularly important for small firms. A small firm may minimize its investment in fixed assets by renting or leasing plant and equipment, but there is no way it can avoid an investment in cash, receivables, and inventories. Therefore, current assets are particularly significant for the financial manager of a small firm. Further, because a small firm has relatively limited access to the long term capital markets, it must necessarily rely heavily on trade credit by increasing current liabilities. Relationship between Sales, Growth and current Assets The relationship between sales growth and the need to finance current assets is close and direct. For example, if the firms average collection period is 40 days and if its credit sales are 1,000 a day it will have an investment of 40,000 in accounts receivable.

If sales rise to 2,000 a day' the investment in accounts receivable will rise to 80,000. Sales increases produce similar immediate needs for additional inventories and, perhaps, for cash balances. All such needs must be financed, and since they arise so quickly, it is imperative that the financial manager keep himself aware of developments in the working capital segment of the firm. of course, continued sales increases will require additional long- term assets, while must also be financed. However, fixed asset investments, while critically important to the firm in a strategic, long –run sense do not generally have the same urgency as do current asset investment The term working capital originated at a time when most industries were closely related to agriculture. Processors would buy crops in the fall, process them, sell the finished product, and end up just before the next harvest with relatively low inventories.

Bank loans with maximum maturities of one year were used to finance both the purchase and the processing costs, and these loans were retired with the proceeds from the sale of the finished products. There fixed assets are shown to be growing steadily over time, While current assets jumps at harvest season, then decline during the year, ending at zero just before the next crop is harvested. Short-term credit is used to finance current assets, and fixed assets are financed with long-term funds. Thus the top segment of the graph deals with working capital.

The figure represents, of course, an idealized situation-current assets build up gradually as crops are purchased and processed, inventories are drawn down less regularly, and ending inventory balances do not decline to zero. Nevertheless , the example does illustrate the general nature of the production and financing process, and working capital management consists of decisions relating to the top section of the graph managing current assets and arranging the short-term credit used to finance them.

## Extending The Working Capital Concept

As the economy became less oriented toward agriculture, the production and financing cycles of typical business changed. Although  seasonal patterns still existed, and business cycles also caused asset requirements to fluctuate, it became apparent that current assets rarely, if ever , dropped to zero. This realization led to the development of the idea of' permanent current assets,'' drawn, it maintains the traditional notion that permanent assets should be financed with long –

term capital, while temporary assets should be financed with short-term credit. The pattern was considered to be desirable because it minimizes the risk that the firm maybe unable to pay off its maturing obligations To illustrate, suppose a firm borrows on a one-year basis and uses the funds obtained to build and equip a plant. Cash flows from the plant (profit plus deprecation) are not sufficient to pay of lone at the end of the year. So the loan, then the firm has problems had the plant been financed with long term debt, however, cash flows would have been sufficient to retire the loan, and the problem of renewal would not have arisen .Thus, if a firm finances long-term assets with permanent capital and short-term assets with temporary capital, its financial risk is lower than it would be if long-term assets were financed with short-term debt.

At the limit, a firm can attempt to match the maturity structure of its assets liabilities exactly. A machine expected to last for five years could be financed by a five-year loan ;a 20-year building could be financed by a 20-year mortgage bond; inventory expected to be sold in 20 days could be financed by a 20-day bank loan ;and so forth.

Actually, of course, uncertainty about the lives of assets prevents this exact maturity matching . We will examine this point in the following sections. Figure-2 shows the situation for a firm that attempts to match asset and liability maturity exactly. Such a policy could be followed, but firms may follow other maturity matching policies if they desire. Figure-3, for example, illustrates the situation for a firm that finances all its fixed assets with term capital but part of its permanent current assets with short-term credit.

Longer term versus Short-term Debt The larger the percentage of funds obtained from long-term sources, the more conservative the firm's working capital policy. The reason for this, of course, is that during times of stress the firm may not able to renew its short-term debt. This begin so, why firms ever use short term.

## Concepts of Working Capital

There are two concepts of working capital- gross and net. l Gross working capital refers to the firm's investment in current assets. Current assets are the assets which can be converted into cash within an accounting year (or operating cycle) and include cash, short-term securities, debtors, (accounts receivable or book debts) bills receivable and stock (inventory). 1 Net working capital refers to the difference between current assets and current liabilities. Current liabilities are those claims which are expected to mature for payment within an accounting year and include creditors (accounts payable), bills payable, and outstanding expenses. Net working capital can be positive or negative. A positive net working capital will arise when current assets.

The two concepts of working capital- gross and net – are not exclusive, rather they have equal significance from the management viewpoint The gross working capital concept focuses attention on two aspects of current assets management; (a) How to optimize investment in current assets? (b) How should current be financed? The consideration of the level of investment in current assets should avoid two dangers points- excessive and inadequate investment in current assets. Investment in current assets should be just adequate, not more not less, to the needs of the business firm. Excessive investment in current assets should be avoided because it impairs the firm's profitability, as idle investment earns nothing. On the other hand, inadequate amount of working capital can threaten solvency of the firm because of its inability to meet its current obligation. It should be realized that the working capital needs of the firm may be fluctuating with changing business activity. This may cause excess or shortage of working capital frequently. The management should be prompt to initiate an action and correct imbalances. Another aspect of the gross working capital points to the need of arranging founds to finance current assets. Whenever a need of working capital funds arises due to the increasing level of business activity, or for any others reason, financing arrangement should be made quickly. Similarly, if suddenly, some surplus funds arise they should be allowed to remain idle, but should be invested in short-term securities. Thus the financial manager should have a knowledge of the sources of working capital funds as well as investment avenues where idle funds may be temporarily invested. Net working capital is a qualitative concept. It indicates the liquidity position of firm and suggests the extent to which working capital needs may be financed by permanent sources of funds. Current assets should be sufficiently in excess of current liabilities to constitute a margin or buffer for maturing obligations within the ordinary operating cycle of a business. In order to protect their interests, short-term creditors always like a company to maintain current assets at a higher level than current liabilities. It is a conventional rule to maintain the level of current assets twice the level of current liabilities. However, the quality of current assets should be considered in determining the level of current assets vis'-a-vis' current liabilities. A weak liquidity position poses a threat to the solvency of the company and makes it unsafe and unsound. A negative working capital means a negative liquidity, and may prove to be harmful for the company's reputation. Excessive liquidity is also bad. It may be due to mismanagement of current assets. Therefore, prompt and timely action should be taken by management improve and correct the imbalances in the liquidity position of the firm. Net working capital concept also covers the question of judicious mix of long-term and short-term funds for financing current assets. For every firm, there is a minimum amount of net working capital which is permanent. Therefore, a portion of the working capital should be financed with the permanent sources of funds such as equity share capital, debentures, long-term debt, preference share capital or retained earnings. Management must, therefore, decide the extent to which current assets should be financed with equity capital and/or borrowed capital.

In summary, it may be emphasized that both gross and net concepts of working capital are equally important for the efficient management of working capital. There is no precise way to determine the exact amount of gross, or net working capital for any firm. The data and problems of each company should be analyses to determine the amount of working capital. There is no specific rule as to how current assets should be financed. It is not feasible in practice to finance current assets by short-term source only. Keeping in view the constraints of the individual company, a judicious mix of long and short-term finances should be invested in current assets. Since current assets involve cost of funds, they should be put to productive use.

The common definition and its implications The most common definition of net working capital is the difference between a firm's current assets and current liabilities. As long as firms current assets exceed its current liabilities, it has net working capital. Most firm must operate with some amount of net working capital; now much depends largely on the industry. Firms with very predictable cash flows, such as electric utilities, can operate with negative net working capital; however, most firms must maintain positive levels of net working capital. The theoretical underpinning for the use of net working capital to measure a firms liquidity is the belief that the greater the margin by which a firms current assets cover its short-term obligations (current liabilities) the more able it will be to pay its bill as they come due. However, a problem arises because each current asset and current liability has a different degree of liquidity associated with it. Although the firms current assets may not be converted into cash at precisely the point in time when it is needed the greater the amount of current assets present the more likely it is that some current asset will be converted into cash in order to pay a debt that is due. It is the non synchronous nature of a firms cash flows that makes net working capital necessary. The firms cash outflows resulting from payment of current liabilities are relatively predictable. It generally learns when bills are due when an obligation is incurred. For instance, when merchandise is purchased on credit, the credit terms extended to the firm require payment at a known point in time. The same predictability is associated with notes payable and accruals, which have stated payment dates. What is difficult to predict are the firms cash inflows. Predicting when current assets other than cash and marketable securities will be converted into cash is quite difficult. The more predictable these cash inflows are the less net working capital a firm requires. It is because an electric utility has a very predictable pattern of cash inflows that it can operate with little or no net working capital. Firms with more uncertain cash inflows must maintain levels of current assets adequate to cover current liabilities. It is the inability of most firms to match cash receipts and cash disbursements that makes sources of cash receipts, (current assets) that will more than cover current liabilities necessary. For example, if the GHI Company has the current position given in Table 1, the following situation may exist. All Rs.600 of the firms accounts payable, plus Rs.200 of its notes payable and Rs.100 in accruals, are due at the end of the current period. That this Rs.900 in outlays must be made is certain; how the firm will cover these outlays is not certain,. The firm can be sure that Rs.700 will be available since it has Rs.500 in cash and Rs.200 in marketable securities, which can be easily converted into cash. The remaining Rs.200 must come from the collection of an account receivable and/or the sale of inventory for cash. The firm cannot be sure when either a cash sale or the collection of an account receivable will occur. More uncertainty is associated with the collection of accounts receivable than with a cash sale. Although customers who have purchased goods on credit are expected to pay for them by the date specified in the credit arrangement, quite often they will not pay until a later date. Thus the cash flows associated with the purchases will not occur at the point in time they were expected. Of course, some solution to this dilemma must exist. In order to have a higher probability of having sufficient cash to pay its bills, a firm should attempt to make sales, since in many cases they will result in the immediate receipt of cash and in other cases they will result in accounts receivable which will eventually be converted into cash. A level of f inventory adequate to satisfy the probable demand for the firms products should be maintained. As long as the firm is generating sales and collecting receivables as they come due, sufficient cash should be forthcoming to satisfy its cash payment obligations. The GHI Company can increase the probability of its being able to satisfy its obligations by maintaining of some of these items into cash. The more accounts receivable and inventories there are on hand, the greater the probability that some of these items will be turned into cash. As a rule a certain level of net working capital is often recommended in order to ensure that a firm will be able to pay bills. The GHI Company has $1,100 of net working capital ($2,700-$1,600) which will most likely be sufficient to cover all its bills. Its current ratio of 1.69 ($2,700/$1,600), should provide sufficient liquidity as long as its accounts receivable and inventories are relatively liquid.

An alternate definition of net working capital An alternate definition of net working capital is that portion of a firms current assets financed with long-term funds. This definition can best be illustrated by a special type of balance sheet, like that for the GHI Company presented

**Dividend Decisions**

Once a company has been formed and continues in operation, it should have earnings to retain or to distribute to the owners. This disposition of these earnings is a fundamental problem of financial management. In organizations', which are closely held, the problem is not there because the shareholders run the organisation themselves and can dictate the terms. In large organizations, however, the situation is different. Here the policy concerning the distribution of earnings is normally delegated to the directors of the company by the shareholders. However, they retain the final approval authority and the dividend is paid only after final approval of the shareholders in the Annual General Meeting. Once it is approved in the AGM, the dividend cheque is sent to the shareholders within a month and is normally payable in the city of residence of the shareholder so as to expedite the payment to him.

The management of an enterprise has an important financial decision to decide about the disposition of income left after meeting all business expenses. Generally, of the total business profits, a portion is retained for reinvestment in the business and rest is distributed to shareholders as dividend. Organizations' finance a large portion of their needs internally, that is, from retained earnings and from non-cash charges, such as depreciation, to the extent that they are covered by earnings. To the extent that the organizations' are dependent on internal funds to meet their capital and other requirements, there could be a concern that the funds retained may not be used as productively as they might be elsewhere. In a small concern (especially proprietorship/ partnership) the owners are very likely to compare the return to be gained from retained earnings in the business and the return that they might make from some other investment of equivalent risk. Because they do not participate directly in formulating dividend policy, shareholders in large companies do not have the chance to make this direct comparison. Thus earnings that are retained in many companies have not met a "market test" and therefore we may not be sure that they should have been retained. The objective of the dividend policies should be to divert funds from the less productive operations to more productive ones. But it is very difficult for the directors and the management to accept the fate of a declining company and to allow the gradual liquidation of their company, as would be suggested by economic thought. If the management finds itself in a declining industry, they want to retain more funds for the business operations and pay out less so as to conserve the funds. Something that is not beneficial for the shareholders. They also try to retain more to fund other more profitable investments so the continuity of the corporation can be maintained. The important issue is to decide the portion of profit to declare for dividend pay out and for retaining in business. The dividend policy decision involves two questions:

1 What fraction of earnings should be paid out, on average, over time? And 1 Should the firm maintain a steady, stable dividend growth rate?

Before we try and answer these questions, let us look at the theories related to dividend decisions. After that we will look at the empirical evidence of the same. Theories of Dividends

Traditional Position: MM Model

Dividend Irrelevance: Miller and Modigliani

Miller and Modigliani developed the dividend irrelevance theory, which holds that a firm's dividend policy has no effect either on the value of the firm or on its cost of capital (Do you remember the capital structure theories?). MM used the same five assumptions as they used in the debt policy:

1. There are no personal or corporate income taxes.

2. There are no share floatation or transaction costs.

3. Investors are indifferent between a rupee of dividends and a rupee of capital gains.

4. The firm's capital investment policy is independent of its dividend policy.

5. Investors and managers have the same set of information (symmetric information) regarding future investment opportunities.

The above assumptions that give us MM1 actually yield a far more powerful result than just the irrelevancy of debt policy. They imply that the entire financial policy followed by the organisation is irrelevant for its valuation; all that matters is the organization's portfolio of investment projects. Hence, capital structure, dividend policy and risk management activities (among other things) are all ineffectual in altering organization's value.

Consider a firm that has fixed its investment policy. In each period, it is left with a net cash flow, which is simply the difference between operating income and investment costs. A straightforward corporate dividend policy would just be to pay out this net cash flow to the holders of the equity. However, consider a firm that desires to pay a dividend in excess its cash flow. In order to do this, the firm can raise funds by issuing new equity. Alternatively, the firm could borrow money, which assuming perfect capital markets is a transaction with the NPV of zero. Conversely, a firm wishing to pay a smaller dividend might spend the balance of its net cash flow on repurchasing equity. The key idea here is that a firm can choose whatever pay-out policy it desires, funding the policy through share issues/ repurchases; hence; dividend policy is irrelevant.

In other words, they reasoned that the value of a firm is determined by its basic earning power and its risk class, and, therefore, that a firm's value depends on its asset investment policy rather than on how earnings are split between dividends and retained earnings. MM demonstrated, under the light of above mentioned assumptions, that if a firm pays higher dividends, then it must sell more shares to new investors, and the value of the shares given to the new investors is exactly equal to the dividends paid out.

From the individual investor's point of view we can show that the dividend policy is irrelevant too. To do this we can use a similar argument to that employed when we said that shareholders are indifferent to capital structure changes; shareholders are indifferent to dividend policy as, through appropriate purchases or sales of shares, they can replicate any dividend policy they wish. Hence, investors will not value a firm paying a particular dividend policy different to any other firm such that firm value does not depend on dividends.

The MM assumptions are not realistic, and they obviously do not hold precisely. Firms and investors do pay income taxes, firms do incur floatation costs, and investors do incur transaction costs. Further, managers often have better information than outside investors. Thus, MM's theoretical conclusions on dividend irrelevance may not be valid under real-world conditions.

## Radical Models

Bird-in-the-hand Theory: Gordon and Lintner Gordon and Lintner argue that the cost of equity increases as the dividend payout is reduced, because investors can be more sure of receiving dividends than the capital gains that are expected to result from retained earnings. Therefore, the theory holds that the value of the firm will be maximised by a high dividend payout ratio, because investors regard actual dividends as being less risky than potential capital gains.

This means that this theory is in direct contrast with MM theory of dividend irrelevance. Tax Preference Theory: Litzenberger and Ramaswamy If a firm retains its earnings then the share gains in value in the market which results in capital gains for the shareholder. If the company pays out dividend the share value does not increase but the shareholder gains cash. In case of getting dividends the shareholder has effectively paid only 10% tax while in the case of capital gains he would be in the 20% tax bracket. This means that he would prefer to get dividends rather than get capital gains but if the capital gains are disproportionate he would prefer capital gains rather than dividends. The tax preference theory holds that the value of the firm will be maximised by a low dividend payout, because investors pay lower effective taxes on capital gains than on dividends internationally. In India the situation is different and the shareholder would prefer dividends rather than capital gains. The above analysis suggests that there is a preference for current dividends - that, in fact, there is a direct relationship between the dividend policy of a firm and market value. The argument goes on the lines that investors are generally risk averse and therefore attach less risk to current as opposed to future dividends or capital gains. In the words of John E. Kirshmann "Of two stocks with identical earnings, records and prospects but the one paying a larger dividend than the other, the former will undoubtedly command a higher price merely because shareholder's prefer present to future values. Myopic vision plays a part in the price-making process. Stockholders often act upon the principle that a bird in hand is work two in the bush and for this reason are willing to pay a premium for the stock with the higher dividend rate, just as they discount the one with the lower dividend rate."

Benjamin Graham and David L. Todd, authors of the well-known security valuation book 'Security Analysis' also say that "The typical investor would most certainly prefer to have his dividend today and let tomorrow take care of itself. No instances are on record in which the withholding of dividends for the sake of future profits has been hailed with such enthusiasm as to advance the price of the stock. The direct opposite has invariably been true. Given two companies in the same general position and with the same earnings power, the one paying the larger dividend will always sell at the higher prices."

These observations are supported by the share valuation models that have been developed using the dividend payouts. Walter's model (which is actually an adaptation of the Gordon's model) are given below.

## Walter's Model

Walter's model is one of the earliest dividend models is adapted from the Gordon's model for valuation of an equity share. Gordon's model gives us the cost of internally generated common equity,

$$ks = \frac{\text{dividend in year 1}}{\text{market price}} + \left( \begin{array}{c} \text{annual growth} \\ \text{in dividends} \end{array} \right)$$

$$ks = \frac{D_1}{P_o} + g$$

which can also be written as:

$$P_0 = \frac{D_1}{K_s - g}$$

Hence the dividend growth rate can be subtracted from the cost of equity capital to get the present value of the share price which should be the market price according to the formula.

Walter adjusted the above formula to reflect the earnings retention and rewrote the equation as:

$$P_0 = \frac{D_1}{K_s - rb}$$

Here, b is the percentage of earnings retained, and r is the expected rate of profitability from the retained earnings.

It follows from the formula that if the earnings retained gives you a higher return than the cost of capital, you would get a positive return and the share price would go up and otherwise the share price would come down because of the higher earnings retained.

Walter's formula highlights the return on retained earnings relative to the average market rate of return on investment (market capitalisation rate) as the critical determinant of dividend policy. A high rate of return on retained earnings indicates a low payout ratio, whereas a low rate relative to the market average indicates the desirability of a high payout ratio to increase the price of the equity shares.

Therefore to increase the share valuation a company may go in for a higher payout in the form of a dividend. But this reduces the growth rate of the dividends (keeping all other things constant) bringing it back to square one. Also a high dividend policy may force the firm to go to the capital markets more often. In practice, most firms try to follow a policy of paying a steadily increasing dividend.

This policy provides investors with stable, dependable income, and if the signaling theory is correct, it also gives investors information about management's expectations for earnings growth.

Most firms use the residual dividend model to set a long run target payout ratio which permits the firm to satisfy its equity requirements with retained earnings.

## Factors Affecting Dividend Policies

**Fund Requirements:** Generally, the firms that have substantial investment opportunities and consequently considerable funding needs to keep their payout ratio rather low to conserve resources for growth. On the other hand, firms which have rather limited investment avenues usually pursue a more generous payout policy.

**Bond in dentures:** Debt contracts often restrict dividend payments to earnings generated after the loan was granted. Also, debt contracts frequently stipulate that no dividends can be paid unless the current ratio, the interest coverage ratio, and other safety ratios exceed stated minimum values. Preference share restrictions: Typically, equity dividends cannot be paid if the company has omitted (not paid) dividend on its preference shares. The preference dividends arrears must be paid before equity dividends can be resumed.

**Availability of cash:** Cash dividends can only be paid with cash. Thus, a shortage of cash in the bank can restrict dividend payments. However, unused borrowing capacity can offset this factor.

**Control:** If the management is concerned about maintaining control, it may be reluctant to sell new shares, hence it may retain more earnings than it otherwise would. This factor is especially important for small, closely held firms. Differences in the cost of External equity and Retained Earnings: Cost of external equity is obviously more than the cost of retained earnings due to the floatation costs of raising the former. Therefore, if the company has some expansion plans which involves capital expenditure it is very likely that it would prefer a low dividend payout ratio. Signalling: As we have noted earlier, managers can and do use dividends to signal the firm's situation. For example, if management thinks that investors do not fully understand how well the firm is doing, and how good its prospects are, it may increase the dividend by more than that was anticipated in an effort to boost the stock price.

**Shareholder Preference:** When equity shareholders have greater interest in current dividend vis-a-vis capital gains, the firm may be inclined to follow a liberal dividend payout policy. While the preference of equity shareholders has some influence over the dividend policy of the firm, the dividend policy may have a greater impact on the kind of shareholders who are attracted towards it. Each firm is likely to draw itself a "clientele" which finds its payout policy attractive.

As mentioned above certain formal and casual empirical observations point in the opposite direction. Perhaps the most famous set of results on actual dividend policy was compiled and presented by John Lintner. Lintner interviewed the management of a sample of US corporations in order to determine what lay behind their dividend-setting decisions. His research led to the four following stylised facts: l Managers seem to have a target dividend pay-out level.

l This pay-out level is determined as a proportion of long run (i.e. sutainable) earnings of the firm. l Managers are more concerned with changes in dividends rather than the actual level of dividends. l Managers prefer not to make dividend changes that might need to be reversed (e.g. cutting dividends after having raised them in the previous period).

As the second fact implies, it is not current but long-run earnings that matter in setting dividends such that dividends can be seen to be smoothed relative to earnings. There are three basic types of dividend policies that are used by the companies. They are

1. Stable dividends

2. Target Payout Ratio and

3. Regular and extra dividends

**1. Stable dividends:** A company following this type of a policy maintains a constant dividend rate irrespective of the actual earnings level and the company tries to maintain it even when during the recession the earnings go down below the actual dividends pay, trying to signal to the investor that this is a temporary phase and earnings will be back up when the economy revives. Companies expect that the investors will place a premium on the shares of a company which pays stable dividends and only increases its dividend payment when it believes that increase can be maintained. A stable dividend policy irrespective of fluctuating earnings also is beneficial because many institutions take decisions based on the actual payout by the companies. Signalling effect of this type has already been mentioned above.

This is the most favoured type of dividend policies adopted by the companies the world over.

**2. Target Payout Ratio:** Although there is a reason to believe that stable dividends have a positive effect on a company's share price, many firms set a bench-mark target payout ratio (or range). They only deviate from this target to achieve relatively stable dividends or stable and occasionaly increasing ones. Lintner contents that companies seek to maintain a target dividend payout ratio over the long run, but only with a lag. For example, a company may decide that it will pay around 40 per cent of its earnings as dividends and only increase it when this ratio falls to 30 per cent of the earnings that the company is reasonably sure of. This is especially applicable in case of companies with stable earnings and earnings growth for only they can sustain a target payout ratio in the long run.

**3. Regular and extra dividends:** Especially when a company earns above average earnings because of any reason but which is non-recurring in nature, it proposes a extra dividend over and above the regular dividend it pays. This extra earnings could be due to divestment of a plant or business operations and the company has no possible utilisation of the same. In line with the recommendations that investors like to receive the money back from the company rather than the company utilizing that money in non-business activities, the companies usually return the money back to the shareholders. This labelling of extra dividends or one-time dividends is given to help the investors appreciate the fact that extra dividends are non-recurring in nature and this is the only year this is being paid. There are other ways of returning cash to shareholders and one of the biggest ones is gaining ground in India recently. This is share buyback.

## Stock Dividends and Stock Splits

An integral part of dividend policy of a firm is the use of bonus shares and stock splits. Both involve issuing new shares on a pro rata basis to the current shareholders while the firm's assets, its earnings, the risk being assumed and the investors percentage ownership in the company remain unchanged. The only definite result from either a bonus share or share split is the increase in the number of shares outstanding. Table illustrates their effect on the capitalization of the firm. Part one of the table shows the equity of the balance sheet before the bonus issue and part two after the issue. The effect of share splits is shown in part three.

| | |
|---|---|
| 1. Equity portion before the bonus issue: | |
| Equity share capital (30,000 shares of Rs.100 each) | Rs. 30,00,000 |
| | 7,50,000 |
| Share premium (@ Rs.25 per share) | 62,50,000 |
| | **1,00,00,000** |
| Retained earnings | |
| **Total equity** | |
| 2. Equity portion after the bonus issue (1 : 2 ratio): | |
| Equity share capital (45,000 shares of Rs.100 each) | Rs. 45,00,000 |
| | 11,25,000 |
| Share premium (45,000 shares X Rs.25) | 43,75,000 |

| | |
|---|---|
| Retained earnings (Rs.62,50,000 – 15,000 shares × Rs.125) **Total equity** | **1,00,00,000** |
| 3. Equity portion before the share splits (10 : 1 ratio): Equity share capital (3,00,000 shares of Rs.10 each) Share premium Retained earnings **Total equity** | 30,00,000 7,50,000 62,50,000 **1,00,00,000** |

TABLE Effect of Bonus Shares and Shares Splits

From Table it is clear that a share split is similar to bonus issue from the economic point of view though there are some difference from the accounting point of view. In the equity portion of the firm, a bonus issue reduces the retained earnings and correspondingly increases paid-up equity and share premium, if any, whereas stock/share split has no such effect. The economic effect of both is to increase the number of equity shares outstanding.

As pointed out earlier, no major economic benefit results from bonus shares and share splits. Yes, certain advantages are associated with them. In the first place, the issue of bonus shares / share splits would have the effect of bringing the market price of shares within more popular range as a result of larger number of shares outstanding. The larger number of outstanding shares will also promote more active trading in the shares due to availability of floating stock. Yet another advantage might relate to the informational content of bonus/split announcement. The announcement is perceived as favourable news by the investors in that with growing earnings, the company has bright prospects and the investors can reasonably look for increase in future dividends. Moreover, it enables the conservation of corporate cash. If the bonus share is an effort to conserve cash for profitable investment opportunities, the share prices will tend to rise and the shareholders benefit. However, if the move to conserve cash relates to financial difficulties within the firm, the market price will most likely react adversely.

Finally, bonus / split announcements improve the prospect of raising additional funds particularly through the issue of convertible debentures.

## Repurchase of Stock

As an alternative to paying cash dividends, a company may distribute income to its shareholders by repurchasing its own shares. Assuming that the repurchase does not adversely affect the firm's earnings, the earnings per share on the remaining shares will increase, resulting in a higher market price per share, which means that the capital gains will have been substituted for dividends. A repurchase that is part of capital restructuring is different from a regular repurchase mentioned above. In a capital restructuring repurchase plan asset sales and issuance of debt are used to bring in additional capital and then this capital is distributed to shareholders through a major, one-time share repurchase.

## Disadvantages/ Advantages of Share Repurchases

1. Repurchase announcements are viewed as positive signals by investors because the repurchase is often motivated by management's belief that the firm's shares are undervalued.

2. The shareholders have a choice to sell or not to sell in share repurchase situation. So those who prefer capital appreciation can get the same and those who prefer cash can sell the shares.

3. Repurchase can help reduce the supply of shares in the market, thereby increasing the value of the share.

4. Management dislikes increasing cash dividend as it sends positive signals about future profitability and if the company cannot maintain the same in the future it may result in a sharp fall in the share price. Therefore, if the earnings increase is only temporary then the management may prefer to make the distribution in the form of a share repurchase.

5. It can help in drastically changing the capital structure of the company, which is otherwise very difficult.

There are certain disadvantages too:

1. The shareholder may benefit more from cash dividends than share repurchase if the market discounts the earnings more than a given level.

2. The selling shareholder may lose because of the share repurchase plan as he would get the long term benefit of share repurchase.

3. The company may pay too high a price for share repurchase, resulting in a reduction in value for existing shareholders.

All this means that share repurchases on a systematic, dependable basis is probably not a good idea. However, it can be given careful consideration if the market is not discounting the share in a proper manner and the company has extra cash that it can utilise for the same. Repurchases can be especially valuable to a firm that wants to make a large shift in its capital structure within a short period of time.

## Procedural and Legal Aspects of Dividends

The amount of dividend that can be legally distributed is governed by company law, judicial pronouncements in leading cases, and contractual restrictions. The important provisions of company law pertaining to dividends are described below.

1. Companies can pay only cash dividends (with the exception of bonus shares). Apart from cash, dividend may also be remitted by cheque or by warrant. The same may also be transmitted electronically to shareholders after obtaining their consent in this regard to the bank account number specified by them. The step has been proposed by the Department of Company Affairs to avoid delay in the remittance of dividend.

2. Dividends can be paid only out of the profits earned during the financial year after providing for depreciation and after transferring to reserves such percentage of profits as prescribed by law. The Companies (Transfer to Reserve) Rules, 1975, provide that before dividend declaration, a percentage of profit as specified below should be transferred to the reserves of the company.

a. Where the dividend proposed is up to 10 per cent of the paid up capital, no amount of the current profits need to be transferred.

b. Where the dividend proposed exceeds 10 per cent but not 12.5 per cent of the paid-up capital, the amount to be transferred to the reserves should not be less than 2.5 per cent of the current profits.

c. Where the dividend proposed exceeds 12.5 per cent but not 15 per cent, the amount to be transferred to reserves should not be less than 5 per cent of the current profits.

d. Where the dividend proposed exceeds 15 per cent but not 20 per cent, the amount to be transferred to reserves should not be less than 7.5 per cent of the current profits.

e. Where the dividend proposed exceeds 20 per cent, the amount to be transferred to reserve should not be less 10 per cent.

f. A company may voluntarily transfer a percentage higher than 10 per cent of the current profits to reserves in any financial year provided the following conditions are satisfied:

(i) It ensures that the dividend declared in that financial year is sufficient to maintain average rate of dividend declared by it over three years immediately preceding the financial year.

(ii) In case, it has issued bonus shares in the year in which dividend is declared or in the three years immediately preceding the financial year, it maintains the amount of dividend equal to the average amount of dividend declared over the three years immediately preceding the financial year.

However, maintenance of such minimum rate or quantum of dividend is not necessary if the net profits after tax in a financial years are lower by 20 per cent or more than the average profits after tax of the two immediately preceding financial years.

g. A newly incorporated company is prohibited from transferring more than then percent of its profits to reserves. The 'current profit' for the purpose of transfer to reserves will be profits after providing for statutory transfer to the Development Rebate Reserve and arrears of depreciation if any.

3. Due to inadequacy or absence of profits in any year, dividend may be paid out of the accumulated profits of previous years. In this context, the following conditions, as stipulated by the companies (Declaration of Dividend out of Reserves) Rules, 1975, have to be satisfied.

a. The rate of the declared dividend should not exceed the average of the rates at which dividend was declare by the company in 5 years immediately preceding that year or 10 per cent of its paid-up capital, whichever is less.

b. The total amount to be drawn from the accumulated profits earned in previous years and transferred to the reserves should not exceed an amount equal to one-tenth of the sum of its paid-up capital and free reserves and the amount so drawn should first be utilized to set off the losses incurred in the financial year before any dividend in respect of preference or equity shares is declared. The balance of reserves after such drawl should not fall below 10 per cent of its paid-up capital.

4. Dividends cannot be declared for past years for which accounts have been adopted by the shareholders in the annual general meeting.

5. Dividend declared, interim or final, should be deposited in separate bank account within 5 days from the date of declaration and dividend will be paid within 30 days from such a date.

6. Dividend including interim dividend once declared becomes a debt. While the payment of interim dividend cannot be revoked, the payment of final dividend can be revoked with the consent of the shareholders.

## Procedural Aspects

The important events and dates in the dividend payment procedure are:

1. Board Resolution: The dividend decision is the prerogative of the board of directors. Hence, the board of directors should in a formal meeting resolve to pay the dividend.

2. Shareholder Approval: The resolution of the board of directors to pay the dividend has to be approved by the shareholders in the annual general meeting.

However, their approval is not required in the case of declaration of interim dividend. Further, it should be noted that the shareholders in the annual general meeting have neither the power to declare the dividends

3. Record Date: The dividend is payable to shareholders whose names appear in the register of members as on the record date.

4. Dividend Payment: Once a dividend declaration has been made, dividend warrant must be posted within 30 days. Within a period of 7 days, after the expiry of 30 days, unpaid

dividends must be transferred to a special account opened with a scheduled bank.

In case the company fails to transfer the unpaid dividend to the 'unpaid dividend account' within 37 days of the declaration of dividend, an interest of 12 percent per annum on the unpaid amount is to be paid by the company. The interest so accruing is to be paid to the shareholders in the proportion of the dividend amount remaining unpaid to them.

The dividend will be paid to the registered shareholder or to his order or to his banker or in case a share warrant has been issued to the bearer of such a share warrant. In the case of joint-holders, the dividends should be paid to the first joint holder.

Further, as per the notification issued by the Department of Company Affairs, the payment of dividend to the shareholders involving the fraction of 50 paise and above be rounded off to the rupee and the fraction of less than 50 paise may be ignored.

In the case of dematerialized shares (i.e., the shares held in electronic form), the corporate firms are required to collect the list of members holdings shares in the depository and pay them the dividend.

4. Unpaid dividend: If the money transferred to the 'unpaid dividend account' in the scheduled bank remains unpaid / unclaimed for a period of 7 years from the date of such transfer, the company is required to transfer the same to the 'Investor, Education and Protection Fund' established for the purpose.

## What is Ratio Analysis ?

**Ratio analysis is one of the oldest methods of financial statements analysis**. It was developed by banks and other lenders to help them chose amongst competing companies asking for their credit. Two sets of financial statements can be difficult to compare. The effect of time, of being in different industries and having different styles of conducting business can make it almost impossible to come up with a conclusion as to which company is a better investment. Ratio analysis helps creditors solve these issues. Here is how:

**What are Financial Ratios ?**

- **Shortcut:** Financial ratios provide a sort of heuristic or thumb rule that investors can apply to understand the true financial position of a company. There are recommended values that specific ratios must fall within. Whereas in other cases, the values for comparison are derived from other companies or the same companies own previous records. However, instead of undertaking a complete tedious analysis, financial ratios helps investors shortlist companies that meet their criteria.

- **Sneak-Peek:** Investors have limited data to make their decisions with. They do not know what the state of affairs of the company truly is. The financial statements provide the window for them to look at the internal operations of the company. Financial ratios make financial analysis simpler. They also help investors compare the relationships between various income statement and balance sheet items, providing them with a sneak peek of what truly is happening behind the scenes in the company.

- **Connecting the Dots:** Over the years investors have realized that financial ratios have incredible power in revealing the true state of affairs of a company. Analyses like the DuPont Analysis have brought to the forefront the inter-relationship between ratios and how they help a company become more profitable.

## Sources of Data

Here is where the investors get the data they require for ratio analysis:

- **Financial Statements:** The financial data published by the company and its competitors is the prime source of information for ratio analysis.

- **Best Practices Reports:** There are a wide range of consulting firms that collate and publish data about various companies. This data is used for operational benchmarking and can also be used for financial data analysis.

- **Market:** The data generated by all the activity on the stock exchange is also important from ratio analysis point of view. There is a whole class of ratios where the stock price is compared with earnings, cash flow and such other metrics to check if it is fairly priced.

## Techniques Used in Ratio Analysis

Ratio, as the name suggests, is nothing more than one number divided by the other. However, they become useful when they are put in some sort of context. This means that when an analysts looks at the number resulting out of a ratio calculation he/she must have a reasonable basis to compare it with. Only when the analyst looks at the number and compares it what the ideal state of affairs should be like, do the numbers become powerful tool of management and financial analysis.

**Dividing numbers and obtaining ratios is therefore not the main skill.** In fact this part can be automated and done by the computer. Companies wouldn't want to pay analysts for doing simple division, would they?. **The real skill lies in being able**

**to interpret these numbers**. Here are some common techniques used in the interpretation of these numbers.

## Horizontal Analysis

Horizontal analysis is an industry jargon for comparison of the same ratio over time. Once a ratio is calculated, it is compared with what the value was in the previous quarter, the previous years, or many years in case the analyst is trying to make a trend. This provides more information of two grounds. They are:

- Horizontal analysis clarifies whether the company has a stable track record or is the value of the ratio influenced by one time special circumstances.
- Horizontal analysis helps to unveil trends which help analysts unveil trends in the performance of the business. This helps them make more accurate future projections and value the share correctly.

## Cross-Sectional Analysis

Cross sectional ratio analysis is the industry jargon used to denote comparison of ratios with other companies. The other companies may or may not belong to the same industry. Cross sectional analysis helps an analyst understand how well a company is performing relative to its peers. In a way this removes the effect of business cycles. There are many variations of cross sectional analysis. They are as follows:

- **Industry Average:** The most popular method is to take the industry average and compare it with the ratios of the firm. This provides a measure of how the company is performing in comparison to an average firm.

- **Industry Leader:** Many companies and analysts are not satisfied with being average. They want to be the industry leader and therefore benchmark against them.

- **Best Practice:** In case, the company is the industrial leader, then it usually crosses the industry border and seeks inspiration from anyone anywhere in the world. They benchmark with the best practices across the globe.

## Importance of Different Ratios to Different User Groups

As we have seen earlier that there is a wide variety of financial ratios available. They fall into many categories and if variations are included there are hundreds of types of ratios that are common in practice. However, all the ratios are not used by everyone on a regular basis. There are some ratios which are more important to some user groups than they are to other user groups. This explains why this is the case:

## Management: Turnover and Operating Performance Ratios

The management of the company may not be so concerned with the results. They are usually more interested in the cause. This is because while other classes of stakeholders do not have control over the working of the firm i.e. the cause, the management does. All the other stakeholders question the management at the annual general meeting. Hence, management tries to get as much insight into the ratios as possible. They create operating performance ratios and compare it to their previous performance and to the performance of others to learn from the past as well as to be able to give satisfactory answers to the investors.

## Shareholders: Profitability

Shareholders, for obvious reasons, are most concerned about profitability. Their investments are at risk and they expect to gain the maximum. Investors scrutinize profitability numbers and pounce upon the slightest signs of mismanagement. For the shareholders, the profitability ratios are the beginning point. They then follow the trail the ratios leave. However over the past two decades the focus has been steadily shifting towards cash flow ratios.

### Debt holders and Suppliers: Cash Flow and Liquidity

Debt holders and suppliers are concerned whether they will be paid the amount promised to them at the date that was promised to them. It is for this reason that they are very concerned about the liquidity of the firm. Slightest signs of liquidity issues are met with supply cutbacks from suppliers.

The fact that debt holders are concerned about the same ratios creates a self reinforcing negative loop for the company. This is because at the same time when suppliers cut credit and supplies, debt holders refuse to lend more money and the whole situation becomes a cash crunch.

### Credit Rating Agencies: Solvency

While debt holders are suppliers are concerned about short term liquidity and cash flow, credit rating agencies go a step ahead. They use solvency ratios to rigorously analyze whether the company will be able to make good its obligations in the long run.

## Limitations of Ratio Analysis

Ratio analysis, without a doubt, is amongst the most powerful tools of financial analysis. Any investor, who wants to be more efficient at their job, must devote more time towards understanding ratios and ratio analysis. However, this does not mean that it is free of limitations. **Like all techniques, financial ratios have their limitations too. Understanding the limitations will help investors understand the possible shortcomings with ratios and avoid them**. Here are the shortcomings:

## Misleading Financial Statements

The first and foremost threat to ratio analysis is deliberate misleading statements issued by the management. The management of most companies is aware that investors look at certain numbers like sales, earnings, cash flow etc very seriously. Other numbers on the financial statements do not get such attention. They therefore manipulate the numbers within the legal framework to make important metrics look good. This is a common practice amongst publically listed companies and is called "Window Dressing". Investors need to be aware of such window dressing and must be careful in calculating and interpreting ratios based on these numbers.

## Incomparability

Comparison is the crux of ratio analysis. Once ratios have been calculated, they need to be compared with other companies or over time. However, many times companies have accounting policies that do not match with each other. This makes it impossible to have any meaningful ratio analysis. Regulators all over the world are striving to make financial statements standardized. However in many cases, companies can still choose accounting policies which will make their statements incomparable.

## Qualitative Factors

Comparison over time is another important technique used in ratio analysis. It is called horizontal analysis. However, many times comparison over time is meaningless because of inflation. Two companies may be using the same machine with the same efficiency but one will have a better ratio because it bought the machine earlier at a low price.

Also, since the machine was purchased earlier, it may be closer to impairment. But the ratio does not reflect this.

## Subjective Interpretation

Financial ratios are established "thumb of rules" about the way a business should operate. However some of these rules of thumb have become obsolete. Therefore when companies come with a new kind of business model, ratios show that the company is not a good investment. In reality the company is just "unconventional". Many may even call these companies innovative. Ratio analysis of such companies does not provide meaningful information. Investors must look further to make their decisions.

## Degree of Financial Leverage Ratio

A high debt equity ratio makes the company financed by debt more than by equity. Therefore there are fixed interest payments involved. Hence when the going is good, the company makes a handsome return as a small percentage of change in EBIT creates a large percentage change in earnings per share. However the inverse of this is also true. Just like financial leverage helps to magnify profits, it also magnifies losses when EBIT fall down. Analysts want to quantify exactly how much variability does debt funding create in the operations of a particular company and have created a measure called "Degree of Financial Leverage" which we will study in detail.

**Formula**

**Degree of Financial Leverage = % Change in EPS / % Change in EPS**

There is a reasonable assumption about the absence of any changes in accounting policy which would make the EPS and EBIT figures incomparable from the previous years.

**Example**

- **Profit Magnification Example:** The best example of degree of financial leverage is in the field of home ownership. Let's say that you brought a house for Rs 100. It is financed 30% by own money and 70% by debt bearing interest of 10%.

Thus, you are obligated to pay Rs 7 interest each year, regardless of what happens. Lets say that the price of the house went up by 20% to 120. In this case you will pay back the creditors Rs 77 (principal + interest) and be left with Rs 43. Since your original investment was Rs 30, you have gained Rs 13.

A price increase of 20% has led to an increase in the shareholders return by approximately 43%!

- **Loss Magnification Example:** Let's say that you brought the same house for Rs 100. It is financed 30% by own money and 70% by debt bearing interest of 10%.

Thus, you are obligated to pay Rs 7 interest each year, regardless of what happens. Lets say that the price of the house went down by 20% to Rs 80. In this case you will pay back the creditors Rs 77 (principal + interest) and be left with Rs 3. Since your original investment was Rs 30, you have lost Rs 27.

A price decrease of 20% has led to a decrease in the shareholders return by approximately 90%

## Interpretation

Leverage is very dangerous unless the company is reasonably certain of its earnings. Investors view the leverage ratio with great detail. This is because it enables a small change in the EBIT to completely wipe out the company's capital and make it insolvent almost overnight.

## Degree of Operating Leverage Ratio

The degree of operating leverage of a company is very important from an investor's standpoint. Although it shows the riskiness of a venture, it also shows the efficiency of a company. Just like, financial leverage arises out of the capital structure of a company, operating leverage arises out of its cost structure. If a company has too many expenses which are fixed in nature, the company is said to have high operating leverage.

Typically companies that are highly mechanized have high operating leverage. This is because they have replaced labor which is a variable cost by depreciation on machinery which is a fixed cost. This creates debate whether having a high operating leverage is a bad thing. Henry Ford was amongst the first to use operational leverage on a large scale and build cars at a fraction of what it would cost earlier. This idea was soon followed by many others and high operating leverage became the norm.

## Formula

## Degree of Financial Leverage = % Change in Sales / % Change In EBIT

The ratio makes a reasonable assumption that accounting policies have not changed so much that the Sales and EBIT figures do not remain comparable across companies or across time.

## Example

- **Profit Magnification Example:** In case a company has a high operating leverage, most of its costs are fixed. Consider for example, the movie business. The costs incurred to make the movie are fixed. Hence when tickets are sold, the first few tickets go towards recovery of the cost of production. However, once a breakeven point has been reached, entirely all the money goes towards the bottom line. Hence a slight change in sales has the capability to magnify and bring about a big change in EBIT.

- **Loss Magnification Example:** However, every lever has its flipside and operating leverage is no exception. Since most of the costs are fixed, in the vent of a downturn, the company does not have the opportunity to cut costs. In many cases, companies are not able to fulfill their requirements to meet the fixed cost obligation. Whereas all companies are hurt in the event of a downturn, companies with excessively high operating leverage are wiped out in such events.

## Interpretation

Whether operating leverage is good or bad for a company depends on the nature of its operations and stability of its cash flow streams. In case of stable operations, high operational leverage in desirable and even recommended.

## Degree of Combined Leverage Ratio

Most firms use both operating leverage and capital leverage to some extent. In today's business world it is almost impossible to run a business without having some degree of automation and mechanization (operating leverage). It is also not possible to grow at an adequate speed unless the company is taking advantage of borrowed money.

However, the degree to which a company uses

operating leverage and financial leverage can be different. Some companies use more financial leverage than operating leverage while other use more operating leverage. This creates a challenging scenario whereas an analyst has to interpret the different degrees of riskiness of companies with different cost and capital structures. The degree of combined leverage (DCL) makes it possible to do this.

## Formula

- **Degree of Combined Leverage = %Change in EPS / %Change in Sales**
- **Degree of Combined Leverage = Degree of Operating Leverage * Degree of Financial Leverage**

## Example

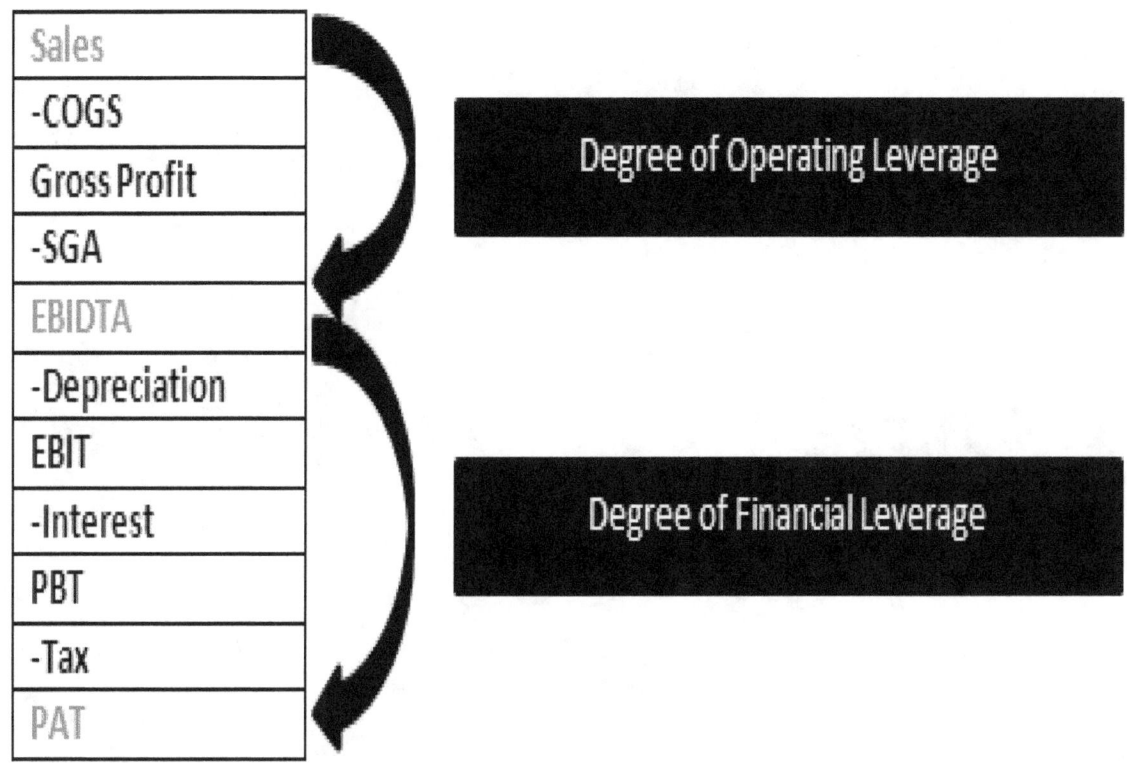

**PAT / Number of Shares = Earnings per Share (EPS)**

Therefore if operating leverage of a firm= 1.4 whereas financial leverage = 2, then the degree of combined leverage equals 1.4*2 = 2.8

## Interpretation

Degree of operating leverage shows how a change in sales affects the EBIDTA of the firm. Whereas degree of financial leverage shows how a change in EBIDTA affects the EPS of the firm. Combining the two analysts can predict how a change in sales is likely to magnify the gains or losses to the EPS.